Introduction

Job interviews are the most crucial part of the hiring process. It is an opportunity the applicant to sell themselves as to why they are a good fit for the company and also to finally decide if the company values align with their own. It can be a scary but rewarding experience, no matter the outcome.
Going into it, there are many things you need to remind yourself of, What to bring, do and say when you're speaking with the employer.
Then there is audacious task of managing the nerves that makes you want to puke up the mcdonalds breakfast you hurriedly ate at the drive thru as you drove to your interview. I wish they had a nerves-resistant happy meal that gives you superpowers and guarantees you the job.

At the time of writing this book, that kind of meal only exist in my head and not on the mcdonald's menu, wait before you close the book and go grumbling with your dissapointed self....wink wink

The information in this book is better than a happy meal, because you can always come back and eat it again and again...more like buy a happy meal once and never pay again but you have the constant companion of never ending nuggets and fries.

This book will ensure that you go in and get it. It will help you collect the necessary documents, as well as get yourself together and make the best of a job interview.

Chapter 1
Preparing for a Job Interview
"Give me six hours to chop down a tree and I will spend the first four sharpening the axe." - Abraham Lincoln

It is completely natural to feel nervous before a job interview, I mean even Beyonce still gets the shivers before an album release meeting. I'm not trying to make you feel better, it's the truth. Go watch her YEAR OF 4 documentary, and no I am not an affiliate.

Preparation is the antidote to nerves.

I wish I could tell you now that you wouldn't feel no nerves but that would be a big fat lie but you can

minimize pre-interview jitters with some preparation. Hopefully you have completed initial research on the company you applied for before being called in for an interview but you are going
to need to do more. You will never know exactly what is going to be asked of you (unless you have an inside source), but you can be ready for the questions by stalking the hiring manager (don't ever do that) I mean stalking the company's website and social media platforms.

Look up the company website and study the history, about us page, and the products and services that are offered. Even if you are pretty sure you are not going to be quizzed on how the company came to be, it will give you insight into how the company operates, their philosophy and culture.

These factors should influence how you answer your questions. If it is obvious they place high value on team players, you should brainstorm and write down situations when you have displayed this trait, not necessarily in a work setting but in regular everyday life.

If you are applying for a sales position, you can be prepared for any role playing questions because you have taken the time to learn the company's products and services.

It will be impressive to your interviewer that you have taken the time to research the information. It shows a commitment to details and a true interest in the company.

Another way to prepare for an interview is to complete a practice run with a friend or family member. Have them ask you questions and answer them as if you were already in the interview, don't break character during the role play either. There are many questions that are asked in a typical interview (what are your strengths and weaknesses) don't let them come as a surprise to you – practice so you can answer with confidence.

What to Wear to a Job Interview

If you are anything like me, possibly even more stressful than the questions you are going to have to answer, is conquering the tedious task of finding the perfect outfit to wear to a job interview. You want to look professional and a culture fit within the company. This is the one and only time I wish I was a man, just because there is no such thing as them overdressing for the interview. A shirt and tie or a suit is always a safe choice. For women, picking the clothes is more challenging.

For both men and women, the only rule is to pick an outfit that you feel comfortable in and that fits properly. You don't want pants that are too tight or a shirt that is too snug across the chest except your intention is to seduce the interviewer, It will be a distraction for both you and your interviewer. Along the same vein, pick colors that suit you but aren't too bright or patterns that are overly bold. You want the focus to be on your answers, not what you are wearing.

They never tell you this but having worked in HR, your overall appearance is going to be judged, and this includes more than the clothes you are wearing. Hygiene and grooming: be clean, neat and tidy.

It is probably best not to wear a strong scent – chances are you will be in a small room and it could make others uncomfortable. Your fingernails should be short and clean, your hair clean and tidy, and have mints with you or brush your teeth immediately before leaving for the interview, your teeth is going to be your most powerful accessory.

You may wonder what all of these details has to do with your qualifications and getting the job. It has to do a lot with it, especially if you are going to be working in a customer facing role.

Chapter 2
THE S.H.A.K.E principle.

The S.H.A.K.E principles are steps I have used personally time and time again to landing the roles of my choice. If you invite me for an interview, best believe I will get the role and it will definitely work for you. This simple yet powerful steps, if properly applied, you will to have your interviewer drooling over you contract in hand saying sign here please.

S- Smile, Speak confidently, Specific answers
H- Honesty
A- Assume not, Ask questions, Answer positively
K- Keen Interest
E- Etiquette, ENTHUSIASM

S- Smile, Speak confidently, Specific answers.

Who isn't nervous during a job interview? Me! What? I just told a lie in a book that will live on the internet forever. The truth is even the most self-assured candidate is going to have a moment or two of self-doubt. My mantra in the moments confidence does a runner on me is to smile and make the switch internally to Godfidence.

A Smile is a powerful universal language that everyone understands and if accessorised properly can portray an image of confidence. This is what a potential employer wants to see, if you are not confident in your own abilities why should they be. Here are a few ways to exude confidence.

Make eye contact, nothing is more of a dead giveaway of poor self-confidence than a person that will not look someone in the eye. Walk up to your interviewer, extend your hand and look in them in the eye when you greet them and express your pleasure of meeting them. And don't beat around the bush when you are talking. Saying things like,

"Well, I kind of helped with a project but I didn't run it myself," screams I do not think I am worthy of this position. Instead, say this,

"I assisted in a very successful project and played a key role in bringing it to completion."

Your role in the project may not have changed the perception the interviewer has of you has.

If you haven't been on very many interviews or it has been some time since you last attended one, it is understandable to be nervous. The more interviews you complete, the more confidence you will gain in your abilities to sell yourself. The fact is that you were selected from a pool of several other candidates and if you were not qualified you would not have gotten the interview in the first place. Use that knowledge to your advantage and instill confidence in yourself.

I personally think of my interview as a red carpet moment and i am the celebrity. I have the opportunity to shine and create a lasting impression.

As a backup measure, get some friends or family members to remind you of all of your great traits and what makes you special – an ego boost before an interview can certainly boost your confidence level.

Make a Connection

Depending on how popular or sought after the job you are interviewing for is you will have a lot of competition for a few positions. A stellar interview is crucial to make you stand out from the rest of the crowd. To give yourself an added edge and cement yourself in your interviewer's mind, try to make a personal connection with them at some point in the interview.

A personal connection can take numerous forms. If you are in the interviewer's office and they have a picture of a sailboat on their wall (and you happen to love sailing), make an appropriate comment that identifies you as a sailor too. This may not put you above others more qualified than you but it will help you to stand out amongst those you are in direct competition with.

Take your cues from the interviewer by observing not just what they say but their body language as well, if they seem uncomfortable with relaying any personal information or are not comfortable veering off topic then follow their lead. If a personal conversation does develop, let the interviewer guide it. When they bring it to a close and either get back to the questions or say goodbye, leave it at that.

At the end of the day, interviewers want to hire people that are qualified and who will fit in with the rest of the team at the company. If you can make a connection and have the right skill sets you will be giving yourself a better chance than someone else. You will also help the interviewer recall who you are and stick out in their mind as that candidate who knew a lot about sailing.

If you are not comfortable with discussing personal topics during an interview, don't feel that you must go out of your way to do so. At the end of the day, your qualifications are what you should be highlighting.

Be Specific when Answering Questions

Sometimes – or more like every time – you go for an interview, your nerves make it can in the way, making it hard to concentrate and answer questions to the best of your ability. The important thing to remember is to really listen to the questions being asked. If the interviewer tells you they want a specific example, don't answer with a general how you would do something – it is a surefire way to ruin your chances for the job, very early on in my job search and interview life, I was lucky to have received this golden nugget as feedback, luckily the interviewer saw past my nerves and still hired me.

These types of questions are known as situational questions. If an interviewer were to say to you,

"Tell us about your favorite vacation."

You wouldn't respond by telling them about all the places you would like to go or make a generalization:

"My favorite vacation is to go someplace hot with my family and sit on the beach."

Instead, you should answer as specifically as possible including all the pertinent details:

"My favorite vacation was two years ago when I went to California with my family. We spent a lot of time on the beach. It was very relaxing."

The second answer adds credibility. It is obvious that you are providing information from something that actually happened as opposed to making something up just to answer the question.

Potential employers are trying to gauge how you react or perform in specific situations. Common questions that are asked include:

"Tell me about a time you led a team project."
Include what the project was, how many people, and any challenges including how you overcame them.

"Tell me about a conflict you had with a co-worker."
Only pick situations that had a positive outcome.

Employers today want to know how you are going to perform on the job before they even hire you. By answering situational questions specifically you can assure the interviewer you have the skills and thought processes that they are looking for.

Be Thorough but to the Point

If you love to talk and when you are nervous can go on and on, or if you are the opposite and clam up when you are in a stressful situation – you need to be conscious of this and not do either in an interview. When asked a question, an interviewer wants enough information that will help them understand what you are talking about, but not extraneous irrelevant information.

If you are answering a question using an example from your previous or current job and there is a lot of jargon or acronyms – try to use more common place term that more people are familiar with or explain what you mean in the beginning. If you are asked to describe a time when you lead a project – explain what the project was about, how many people you managed and any key points that demonstrate what a great job you did. What you don't want to do is get side-tracked and give details that aren't relevant to the question. The interviewer is not going to be interested in a play by play of the entire project – they want to know your role in it.

Keep on topic; take a moment before answering a question to organize the details first in your mind. You don't want to start answering, get sidetracked and forget the point you were trying to make. If you stay on topic and know what you are going to say, you are going to be able to keep the interviewer's attention.

If you are a person of few words, practice with a friend or family member before your interview. Learn how to expand your answers so you give thorough information without living the interviewer wanting more. But if you are in doubt, less is better – an interviewer will ask follow-up questions if necessary.

H- Honesty

There is a difference between telling a story highlighting the positive to make you sound better and lying to the interviewer. It is rare for a company to not conduct reference check these days so don't say anything that can not be verified by your boss or other references that you provide.

There are many ways to get into trouble during an interview and lying is the most severe. Common fibs that are told include educational degrees that you do not hold, saying that you are a manager when really you are a team lead and taking credit for a project that was completed by a coworker. All of these things can make you sound good at the time of the interview, but what if the interviewer talks to your boss about the stellar project you ran for the company when it really wasn't you. Your boss is not going to lie for you and if you were in the running for the job, you won't be anymore.

The best way to handle these scenarios is to tell the truth, put a positive spin on everything including the not so good situations you may have experienced. Employers want to see your vulnerabilities, but it's your job to turn those vulnerabilities into strengths. Maybe you were a part of the project, instead tell the interviewer the part you played and share the success of the project as a whole. An employee that can recognize and share in the success in others is preferable to one who doesn't tell the truth or wants all of the credit for themselves.

Being honest and vulnerable does not mean that you have to share everything including things that doesn't puts you in a negative position. The key is to be honest and only bring up examples that are going to highlight your talents and work history in the best possible way. Don't claim or state anything that cannot be backed up by your references.

Put a Positive Spin on Everything

A potential employer wants to hire people with a positive attitude. You should project this image in your demeanor, facial expressions, and most importantly in the content of your answers. You may be the strongest candidate that the interviewer has seen but you still will not get the job if you are negative and insult former bosses or co-workers or even discredit the last company you worked with.

The best way to do this is to put a positive spin on all of your answers. Most interviews will include a question along one of these lines:

*   Have you had a challenging relationship with a co-worker or boss?
*   What conditions in a workplace make it hard to do your job?
*   How can people tell when you are in a bad mood at work?

Really, all of these are trick questions. What the interviewer really does wants to know is how you have handled conflict in the workplace and how you deal with a bad day at work. They also want to see if you can explain this without being negative, they are also trying to establish your problem solving skills. Even if you have a great story to tell about you and a

co-worker, unless you handled yourself as professionally as
possible and the story portrays you in a positive light do not tell it.

A poor working relationship with your boss may be the reason you are looking for another job in the first place – you and your current boss do not work well together. And good on you for taking charge of the situation to find something that is a better fit for you. But how do you approach this situation so it will not hinder your chances at a new company? There are a few steps you should take first and you need to mind what you say during the interview.

A lot of interviews will contain at least one question about your working relationship with your current boss. They can take many forms and you should prepare for a lot of different types of questions that may be asked. No matter what the question, even if it is one asking you to describe conflict with your boss, be positive and do not bash anyone in your answers.

Remove any emotions from the equation and explain the situation using the facts and highlight all of the professional steps you have taken to rectify the situation. Don't try and make your boss sound like the bad guy, and try to de-emphasize the entire event. It may seem like an opportunity to vent about the

situation but if you do, you are cutting off an avenue to escape the working relationship you want to get away from. Present the
facts, be neutral and highlight your problem-solving skills.

If you are concerned that your current boss will sabotage your efforts to find another job during the reference check stage you can solve this in a couple of ways. If your boss is reasonable and the two of you just don't work well together, chances are you don't have to worry too much. Be sure to give him or her a heads up though. If you aren't comfortable with this, try and find another manager that you have worked for in the company previously that you can pass on as a reference.

If an interviewer asks how co-workers or customers can tell if you are in a bad mood, there is only one right answer, "They can't." You can (and should) elaborate on this, but by answering the question in this vein you are showing that you can leave personal problems and stresses outside the workplace without them affecting your job or others.

Be the kind of person that people want to hire, realistic with an attitude of getting along with others and the ability to get a job done.

A- Assume not, Ask questions, Answer positively

Don't Make Assumptions

This is a good piece of advice to follow in life, but it also has a special place in an interview setting. You want to be viewed as someone who understands what is necessary and can deliver the expected results – more than just in the interview room – and making assumptions will not guarantee you will be viewed like this.

The easiest and best way to avoid assumptions is to ask for clarification. If a question is asked that is ambiguous or you really aren't sure what they mean, ask them to explain it to you. Sometimes, without meaning to, an interviewer will use company jargon or acronyms in a question or in conversation. You can respond by saying,
 "I'm sorry, I'm not familiar with that term, could you explain it to me please?"

Not only will this show that you are paying attention but it will also demonstrate that you have an interest in the company and what they are about.

When you are answering a question and you need to include company specific terminology, be sure to explain what you mean. In addition, you cannot assume that your interviewer will know what you are talking about either. Take a moment to either set up your answer with the required information to understand what you are talking about or pause and explain certain phrases or words. Better yet, if you can use common terms in
the place of company specific ones, it is the preferable way to go.

Lastly, don't assume that the job is in the bag. No matter how confident you are that you are the most qualified person for the position – it isn't yours until you have received a job offer. Make the best impression you have and keep the mindset that you are still competing for the job and sell yourself accordingly.

How to Answer the Tough Interview Questions

Each interview has at least one, question that you really don't know the best way to answer. It is the one that you agonize over for days and keep going over it and over it in your head and you ask others how they would have answered. There is not way to avoid these types of questions but you can answer them with confidence to give yourself peace of mind until you get a call back.

Do not feel that you have to answer immediately after you have been asked a question. You are not on a game show where the fastest contestant to answer wins. Your interviewers will appreciate that you have taken time to formulate your answer. If you are concerned by a prolonged silence – don't be, it is normal. If you have been asked a question that you do not know exactly what to say, ask for a moment to think of an appropriate answer. This is preferable to taking a long time to answer without explaining what you are doing.

If you really can't think of an answer off of the top of your head, ask if you can come back to the question in a moment – keep trying to think of an answer. Don't think that if you get to the end of the interview and you haven't answered the question that you are off the hook. Even if your interviewer doesn't ask again, it has not gone unnoticed that you didn't respond to a question. The best case scenario is for you to bring the topic back to the question and answer it accordingly. Thank your interviewer for giving you the extra time to come up with the right answer.

If it is a lengthy question that is broken into parts, break it down into, don't try and answer it all at once – you can always ask for parts of the question to be repeated.

Answering Unexpected Questions.

You can prepare for an interview until you are blue in the face and still get caught off guard on a question during the process. It is okay, it happens to a lot of people. Some questions come out of left field, sometimes you draw a blank, and others – you really don't know what to say. Here is a brief rundown of what you can do in these three situations.

A (Seemingly) Off Topic Question – These may be thrown in to the interview out of curiosity by the interviewer or to gauge your knowledge on a certain subject. It is not a reason to dismiss the question though and not pay it the care and attention you would to any other one. Do your best, and if you really can't figure out the correlation between the question and the job you are applying to, you can ask at the end of the interview – along the lines, "out of curiosity...."

You Draw a Blank – Ask for a minute to compose your answer, and do some fast brainstorming. If you feel that the silence is becoming uncomfortable, you can ask to come back to the question at the end of the interview. As long as you do go back to it, this is an acceptable solution. Silence is okay during an interview when you are trying to think of an answer, do not feel obligated to fill the silence, concentrate on the answer you want to give.

You Don't Know What to Say – If it is a scenario where you are unsure what the interviewer is looking for in an answer, ask for clarification. Sometimes asking for an example of what they mean can guide you in what you should say. If you take a shot in the dark, you might provide what they want – but why take the chance.

Answering Procedural Questions

Procedures are a part of life, especially in the working world. Each company has their own set of policies and rules that they expect their employees to follow. An interviewer may ask questions to determine if you would do things they way they want (for instance

making a sale or handling a customer complaint). Without training, you will not know with any degree of certainty how the company would want you to handle different
situations but there are ways to answer that can increase your chances of getting the job.

What an interviewer is looking for in an answer is your philosophy towards
circumstances that occur in the company. Your natural instincts and personality is going to come through at some point no matter what you have been trained to do. Questions like,
"How would you satisfy a customer if they wanted to return something after the return policy has expired?" can be tricky to answer. The best way to answer them is to begin with saying,
 "Of course, if hired I would abide by the company's guidelines – but
in this circumstance I would…"

By starting your answer with this phrase you are showing that you recognize a company is going to have its own policies and ways of doing things and that you are flexible enough to modify your way of doing things to align with those processes. Even role playing scenarios for are a test to see if your way of thinking is in line with the company's. This genre of question can backfire on you though if your answer is

completely opposite what the company is looking for. If you have done your research on
the company prior to the interview you should have a good idea of how they handle customers and sales in general.

How to Respond to Taboo Questions

Not all interview questions are acceptable. There are certain topics that should not be brought up and information that a potential employer has no right asking for. Some of these questions are not legal and others while legal may leave you feeling uncomfortable. You do not have to answer certain questions, but how you let the interviewer know this can determine if your application will continue forward.

For more information on questions that should not be asked or that you do not have to answer, contact your local government office that handles labor relations. They can provide these guidelines to you at no cost. If questions are being asked about your private life (and you are uncomfortable answering them), you do not have to. You can mildly tell the interviewer that you plan on devoting the time you spend at work to work and your personal life stays in your personal life. And try to leave it at that. If the interviewer keeps pressing, you will have to decide if the job is worth it to you.

It is your decision to provide the information you do – know your rights beforehand – but you can still decide to answer a question that should not be asked. Keep in mind that if a potential employer wants details about how you spend time outside of work it may be because they expect their employees to put in a lot of extra hours and they are trying to gauge if you have commitments that would prevent you from doing this.

Other questions, such as sexual orientation, past relationships, and other lifestyle choices have no business in an interview setting. If there is a physical aspect to the job and a medical evaluation is necessary, this is typically done by a doctor or other medical professional who will give you clearance. You do not have to provide details to the interviewer.

Pauses and Silences are Okay

There are going to be pauses in conversation or flat out silence during an interview. This can be initiated by you or the interviewer and in most cases either is not an indicator that something is amiss or awkward.

You can ask for a moment to think of an answer and

during this time there is most likely going to be complete silence. This is fine and perfectly normal, don't get distracted because no one is talking, use the time you have asked for wisely and think of the best answer or example you can give.

If the interviewer is taking notes (and most likely they are), be comfortable with the fact that there is going to be pauses in between questions and they try and write everything down. This is actually a good thing because it means they have liked what you have to say and want to remember it when they are later making a decision on who to hire. Don't feel the need to fill this space, let them continue writing and wait for the next question.

If you have answered a question and it is met by silence and the interviewer is not taking notes, you may be at a loss as to what you should do. It could signal that the interview is expecting more information or they are not satisfied with the answer. You won't know unless you ask, "Do you want me to elaborate on that?" If the answer is no, just patiently wait for the next question to be asked. Don't worry that the interviewer is not praising you on your answer to each question and continue onto the next one. They do not want to give you an indication of how you are doing during the interview and are trained to be neutral when responding to answers, if they respond at all.

Explaining Gaps in Employment

Your resume will be the layout for the discussion. In addition to
explaining why you left previous companies and chit chat about the position, if you have any gaps in employment be prepared to explain them. Many people are scared that an interviewer is going to discover that they were without a job for a period of time. It is not necessarily a bad thing, but you do have to be able to tell the interviewer why in the best possible light.

You should always be honest when explaining any absence from working, but you do have a license to spin what you did do in the best possible light. For instance, if you were laid of your job and had a hard time finding a replacement but spent a lot of time with
your children you could say,
 "I took an opportunity to spend a few months with my children in between jobs."
If you took any courses or classes that adds value to your skills as an employee be sure to mention that as well. You may find it beneficial to add a brief explanation on the resume itself or in a cover letter.

Most times it is hard to get to an interview if there is a lengthy and unexplained employment gap.

If you are unsure what possible questions could be generated from your resume, have another person look at it. It is best to be prepared for certain questions and scenarios that will likely come up in an interview. You do not want to be caught unaware or floundering for an answer. Give yourself time to figure out the best explanation for times of unemployment so an interviewer sees it as reasonable or even beneficial to them in the case of additional education and classes.

Ask Your Own Questions

Okay, you have made it to the end of your interview and the interviewer says it is now your turn. They want to know if you have any questions for them. And most likely you do:

"How did I do" and "Are you going to hire me" – unfortunately you can't ask either one. But there are questions that you can ask to glean some information on how you performed and to determine if the company is a right fit for you.

Although it is not acceptable to ask how you did in an interview, it is okay and encouraged to ask what the next steps are and the timeline for them. Depending on how this is answered, you may be able to figure out their reaction to you. But this is not full-proof and is not a guarantee. If they take the time to explain all the checks they need to go through, how many people they have left to interview and so on, they are probably interested and want you to understand that there is still steps left in the process. If they only tell you that you will hear from them within a certain period of time via letter, well it isn't as promising.

Look at the opportunity to ask your own questions as your chance to interview the company. Of course you have done your research prior to attending and have made up a list that you wrote down before attending. Show your preparedness and pull out the list to ask your questions. Things like company direction and expansion show an interest in the business. Feel free to take notes; it can earn you brownie points. Ask questions that
are important to you as well, if vacation time and benefits are a deal breaker for you, find out now what the company has to offer. Here are examples of a few questions you can ask:
1. Tell me about the biggest challenge you think the company will experience this year and how would this position help to overcome it?

2. How do I measure my own performance to ensure that I'm having a positive impact in the role?
3. How did you get hired by the company and what made you decide it is a great place to work?

K- Keen Interest in company

Showing the company that you are interested can oftentimes be subtle. I have been to an interview where the candidates were delayed, I mean three hours delayed most people left and the last person who stayed got the job. The interview was all about patience. It was a start up and all they wanted to know was if the potential candidate would have the patience to go through the growing pains the company was experiencing. I agree that this is very unconventional and contrary to what normal interviews require.

Another way of showing keen interest and respect is by not showing up late for an Interview

This may seem obvious, but it happens way too often. No matter the reason, there is no excuse for it (besides an injury or family emergency and then kudos for you for showing up). Getting lost, bad traffic, or losing track of time doesn't matter to an interviewer. They are taking time away from their primary duties to sit down with you to try and give you a job. It is rude and disrespectful to not show up on time.

Here are a few tips to ensure this doesn't happen:

*   Do a dry run. If you are going to a city or a part of the city you are not familiar with drive there a few days before. Ideally you will do it during a weekday at a similar time to your interview time to gauge the amount of time it takes to get there.
*   Leave early. Not just 15 minutes early, you can plan to arrive 30-60 minutes before your interview time. Don't go into the building though. Get into the area, find a coffee shop and relax while reading the paper or reviewing your resume. Not only will this ensure that you are on time it also gives you time to relax and calm yourself before walking into the building.
*   Pay for parking. Don't circle the block 12 times looking for cheap parking on the street. Pay the money to park in a parking garage. You do not want to waste valuable time looking for parking and start to stress yourself at the same time.

If you are running late (but really, you shouldn't be), make sure you call. The interviewer may not have time to complete the interview if you are running late and you will save both of you the time if you let them know. You can try and salvage the faux pas by trying to book another appointment right away. And if you are lucky enough to get a second chance, follow the tips above to arrive not only on time, but early.

Another way that shows you are interested is to bring doubles of everything to an Interview.

In addition to a list of questions you want to ask and a pen and notepad you should also bring duplicate copies of anything else that you may need to provide to the interviewer. When booking the interview, ask if there is anything specific you should bring with you (normally references is the only requirement). But if you are applying for a driving job, a driver's abstract may be required or if you are applying as a writer you may be asked to
bring in a sample of your work.

Make sure to write down the requested items to bring and make duplicates. If more than one person is going to interview you, bring one for each of them and then one more. This show forethought and preparedness. You also don't want to make your interviewer look bad by not being prepared if they forgot or lost your resume. Let them know that you brought an extra copy for them and hand it over.

Chances are this won't happen, but won't you be happy if it does and you are prepared? By bringing more copies than are required, you can provide your extra copy to the other interviewers so they are not all huddled around the one copy of your writing portfolio or resume.

Even if you are not asked to bring references to the interview, take the time to type out and print copies anyway. If the interview went well you are sure to be asked for them and this again, shows that you think ahead and make the necessary preparations. Do not show up without any special documents that were specifically requested of you, if you do not think you can obtain them in the timeframe given be sure to let the person know before you arrive for the interview.

E- Etiquette, ENTHUSIASM

Etiquette Rules during Job Interviews

During an interview you need to mind your manners and follow a unspoken code of etiquette. This is more than your mom's "keep your elbows off the table." Business manners are going to be key, an interview is so much more than what you have to say – it is how you present (or sell) yourself. If part of the job you are applying for is dealing with clients or executives from other companies, you can be guaranteed how you act is part of the decision making process.

Eye contact- you have to be able to maintain eye contact without being uncomfortable. There are some acceptable ways to do this. If you are answering a question, it is okay to glance away when gathering your thoughts but if you are listening to someone keep your attention focused on them (even if their eyes are wandering). This shows good manners and that you care about what they have to say.

Do not under any circumstances have gum or a mint in your mouth during the interview. If you want to be sure that you have fresh breath, chew gum or suck on the mint before arriving at your destination but discard or finish them before you enter the building. It is distracting and rude to have them in your mouth when answering questions.

Use your interviewer's name, ideally you found out who you would be interviewed by when the meeting was arranged. If it isn't provided to you, be sure to ask who you will be meeting with and their position. When you arrive, shake hands and greet the person by name. If you are just learning their name, repeat it and remember it. You want to be sure to get it right and thank them for their time when you are leaving.

Enthusiasm in a Job Interview

Are you excited at the prospect of getting a new job and are thrilled that you were called in for an interview? Well, then show it when you are being interviewed! Bring an energy and attitude to the interview that will make the company take notice. The process of interviewing is usual a long and boring one for those on the other side of the table. Do your part to make it easier for them to choose you as the best candidate.

Just think of all the people before and after you that are also going to be interviewed for the same position. If all other things were equal – qualifications and the answers to the interview questions – what is going to set you apart from the rest? You can be enthusiastic and smile when answering (when appropriate) and still maintain an aura of professionalism. You want to exude charisma and keep the interviewer's attention. They have heard a lot of the answers already, but you can get the message across with more than words.

Someone who is excited to get a job and lets that excitement be known is going to have a better chance than someone who talks in a monotone and with little to no emotion. Don't be afraid to smile and use phrases as "that's great" or "wonderful" when you are told about the company. Be the type of person that the company wants to represent them and you will increase the chances of a job offer.

A few words of caution: don't go overboard. Be genuine in your enthusiasm and be yourself. Sincerity is key or your enthusiasm could work against you instead of for you. If you are naturally bubbly by nature, tone it down a bit for the interview so you do not overwhelm your hosts.

Chapter 3
The Final Steps

The Panel Interview

An interview can be stressful; you are on display and have to sell yourself as the best candidate for a position in a company. The only thing worse than an interview is the panel interview – when two or more people are asking you questions and watching your every move. This situation may not intimidate everyone, but it is certainly not a comfortable position to be in.

The reason for a panel interview is to get the opinion of multiple people at the same time on the viability of a work candidate. Typically the people that attend are from various departments within the company – a representative from human resources and the department that is hiring at a minimum. This saves time and money for the company and lets them see how the candidates react under pressure.

When you are listening to questions during a panel interview, maintain eye contact with the person who is speaking. Once the question has been asked, make sure to address your answer to all who are present. Make eye contact with everyone and include them in your attention. Be prepared for follow-up questions from any or all of the attendees. Each one is going to want to know information from an angle that will directly affect their
department.

You may find that in some panel interviews, only one person does the talking and everyone else is there simply to observe. Still address all of your comments to the group and don't let this unnerve you. It is definitely stressful, but not unusual. Be flattered that they consider you a strong enough candidate to gather more than one person to evaluate
your interview and choose you to work for the company. An interview is an investment for a company, an expenditure of money in the form of salaries; you are there because you have a chance at the position so take advantage of the opportunity.

Know what Your References are Going to Say about You

Before attending an interview, you should have your references lined-up and ready to provide to the interviewer when asked. More than just writing down names and phone numbers of previous employers and bosses, you need to do additional preparation.

Finding out how a former employer views you and your work history with them is vital before providing that information to a potential employer. Even if your memory of your time spent there is positive, you don't know how you were remembered or what will be said unless you ask.

Your first step should be to contact everyone that you are considering using as a reference. You will want to confirm they are working for the same company and if their phone number is the same. If a boss has moved to another company, you can still utilize them as a reference provided you can track them down. When you reach a potential reference, don't assume they will remember you and everything about you – remind them. Things you say during your conversation can have a positive outcome on what they have to say about you later on. Ask them if they are comfortable providing you with a favorable reference and if there is any feedback they have for you. If you are very comfortable you can flat out ask how they felt about your time working with them and what they would say about you if someone called to ask.

If you are not comfortable with providing a direct supervisor or boss you can use other employees in the company that old a supervisory position. Think of people you have worked closely with on projects or such – they are valid and reputable people to provide as references too.

But if you have made it through the interview process, a reference would have to go quite badly for it to affect a possible job offer.

How to Thank an Interviewer

You may think that it is best to follow-up with an interviewer to thank them for their time and keep your name in the forefront of their mind. While this may have that effect on them, it may not be in the positive way you are looking for. An interviewer takes time out of their regular job to fill vacancies in a department. It is an extremely busy and stressful time for them and they do not want (nor have time to) take calls from everyone that they have completed interviews with.

But this is not to say that sending along a thank you is a bad idea, it's not. The method in which you thank your interviewer is going to make a difference. If you received a business card, send a quick email to thank them for their time and that you are looking forward to hearing from them. Quick and to the point and leave it at that. Do not expect a reply because you probably won't get one and do not follow-up on your e-mail to make sure they received it – you will become an annoyance.

Second to sending a quick e-mail, you can send a short and professional thank you note (this means no scented stationary or something too cutesy). The message should be similar, thanking the interviewer for taking the time to sit down with you, express how much you enjoyed speaking with them and learning more about the company. It is a nicety that while not necessary, can be an added touch to a strong interview.

It may not guarantee you the job, but thank you notes, if done the right way, may open doors for you in the future. If there are openings in the company at a later time, the interviewer may remember you and think of you before others.

How Not to Obsess after a Job Interview

The interview is over and you can't help but sigh with relief. You made it through and it wasn't as bad as you thought it would (or maybe it was, but hey it was a good experience). Now, you might think you are in the clear and all you have to do is wait. While it is true that waiting is the next step, it is not that easy. Some even find it more difficult between the time the interview has been completed to the time they hear back from the company on whether or not they received the position.

Unless you discover that you have given the interviewer misinformation, don't continue to go over your answers again and again. If you look for flaws you will find them. It is unnecessary torture. Keep yourself busy and if you are on a serious job hunt, continue with your search and put the interview on the back burner until you hear back. If you did provide wrong information that would be crucial to a decision you may want to consider
following up to correct the wrong depending on what it was. If it was for a driving job and they asked if you have had any speeding tickets in the past three years and you said yes but later discovered it happened four years ago – definitely call. If on the other hand, you were quoting sales results and underestimated the number of sales you made; it would probably be best left as it was.

Keep yourself busy as you wait for an answer from your interview. And if it happens that you didn't get the job use it as a learning experience. If there were questions you wished you would have answered differently at least you know that now for the next interview you attend.

www.ingramcontent.com/pod-product-compliance
Lightning Source LLC
Chambersburg PA
CBHW031504210526
45463CB00003B/1073